HOW TO MEASURE

Time with a Clock

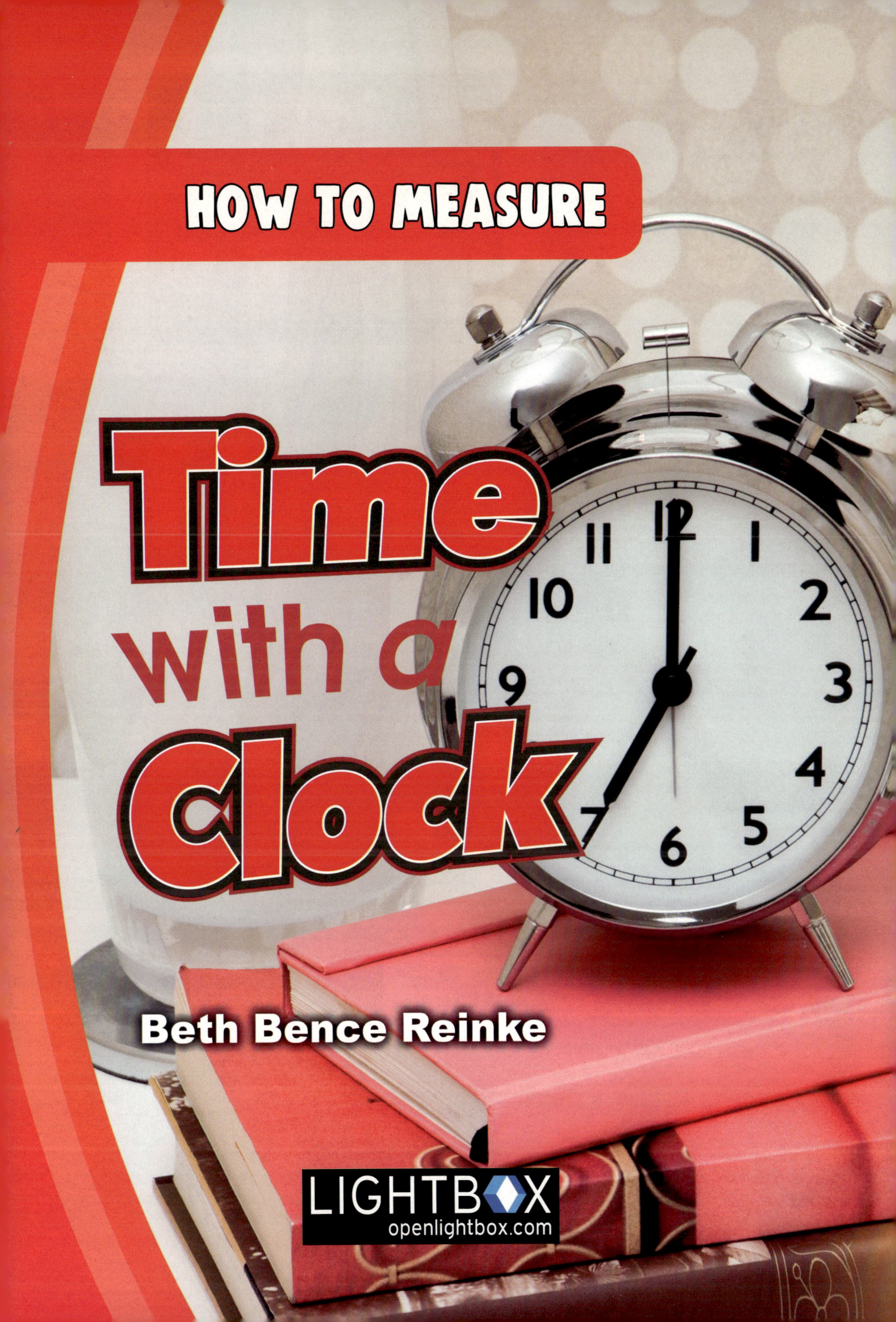

Beth Bence Reinke

LIGHTBOX
openlightbox.com

LIGHTBOX

Go to
www.openlightbox.com
and enter this book's
unique code.

ACCESS CODE

LBD95756

Lightbox is an all-inclusive digital solution for the teaching and learning of curriculum topics in an original, groundbreaking way. Lightbox is based on National Curriculum Standards.

STANDARD FEATURES OF LIGHTBOX

AUDIO High-quality narration using text-to-speech system

ACTIVITIES Printable PDFs that can be emailed and graded

SLIDESHOWS Pictorial overviews of key concepts

VIDEOS Embedded high-definition video clips

WEBLINKS Curated links to external, child-safe resources

TRANSPARENCIES Step-by-step layering of maps, diagrams, charts, and timelines

INTERACTIVE MAPS Interactive maps and aerial satellite imagery

QUIZZES Ten multiple choice questions that are automatically graded and emailed for teacher assessment

KEY WORDS Matching key concepts to their definitions

Contents

Clocks with Hands and Clocks with Numbers

Old-fashioned clocks do not need batteries. They have a spring that is wound for power.

Buzz, buzz, goes Kate's alarm clock. Time to get up! Kate needs to get ready. The school bus will come in half an hour. How many minutes are in half an hour? Measuring time on a clock will help you find out.

Rather than being plugged into the wall, some digital clocks are battery powered. They will keep running if the power goes out.

Clocks with faces and hands are called **analog** clocks. **Digital** clocks have only numbers. Look around. What kinds of clocks do you see?

Hundreds of years ago, people would say it was "**six of the clock**." This was then shortened to "**six o'clock**."

The **largest** clocks in the world are in Saudi Arabia. They are **151 feet** (46 meters) across.

The **smallest** clock in the world weighs **0.04 ounces** (1 gram). That's as much as a **raisin**.

Measuring time helps us keep track of when things happen. What time does the ball game start? How many minutes of recess are left? When is lunchtime?

It helps us know how long things take, too. How many minutes do the cookies bake? How long will you brush your teeth? Let's measure time!

To do the activities in this book, you will need:

- paper plates

- card stock paper

- scissors

- paper fasteners
- markers

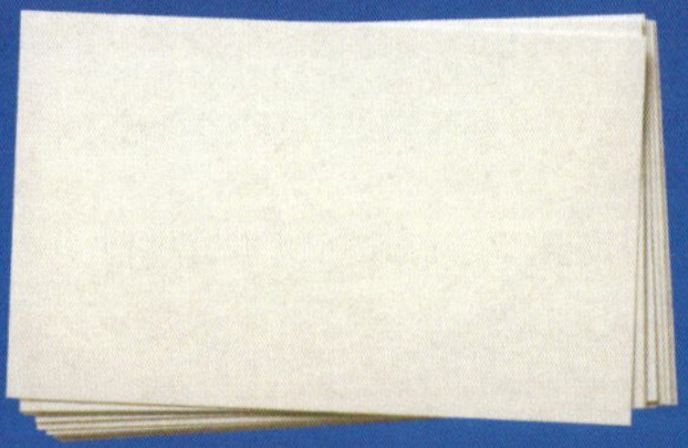

- index cards

Clock Timeline

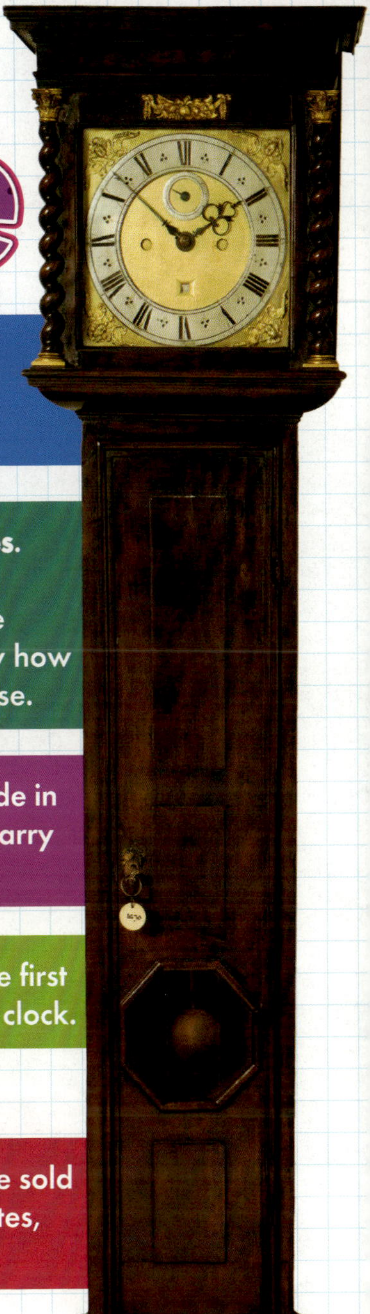

3500 BC Ancient Egyptians build **sundials** to track time. The sun casts a shadow onto the sundial. As the sun moves across the sky, the shadow moves too.

150 BC People first build **hourglasses.** It takes a certain amount of time for sand to trickle from the top to the bottom of the hourglass. Other people measure time by how long it takes to burn candles, oil, or incense.

1510 AD The first pocket watch is made in Germany. It is small enough for people to carry around. However, it is not very accurate.

1895 Frank Hope-Jones of Great Britain invents the first electric clock. Today's clocks are still modeled after this clock.

1990s More than 500 million watches are sold each year. The largest market is the United States, which buys almost 300,000 watches per day.

2015 Apple Inc. releases the Apple Watch. With a "smartwatch," people can now play music, answer calls, and play games.

Units of Time

Juan is making clocks in math class. Each analog clock has two hands. The little hand points to the hour. The big hand shows the minutes. Hours and minutes are **units** for measuring time.

In a single day, all three clock hands overlap 22 times. They cross paths once every 1 hour, 5 minutes, and 27.3 seconds.

There are 60 minutes in one hour. But a clock face has only 12 numbers. On a clock, there are five minutes between each number. How many five-minute blocks are in one hour?

Some clocks show seconds. There are 60 seconds in a minute. The second hand moves really fast!

Most children are taught to tell time with a clock in first or second grade.

Math class is over at nine o'clock. The hour hand points to 9. The minute hand is at 12.

A digital clock shows 9:00. That is another way to say nine o'clock. The hour is on the left of the colon. The minutes are on the right.

Recess begins at 1:00. Kate and Juan play outside for half an hour. The minute hand moves halfway around the clock to the 6. Recess ends at 1:30.

Many people find it easier and quicker to tell time with a digital clock.

Activity

Make Your Own Clock

You can make a clock, too. You can practice telling time.

1 Write the numbers 1 through 12 around the edge of a paper plate.

2 Cut out two hands from card stock paper. Make one hand long and the other short.

3 Poke a hole in one end of each hand. Attach them to the center of the clock with a fastener.

4 Now you can practice. Set the clock to 9:00. Now try 12:00 and 1:30. It's fun to move the hands, isn't it?

5 Practice showing time on the hour. Here are examples: 3:00, 4:00, and 8:00.

6 Now try time on the half hour. Try 2:30, 5:30, and 10:30. Keep practicing!

How Long Does It Take?

Juan rides his bike for an hour. One hour is 60 minutes. The hour hand moves from one number to the next. Juan starts riding at 4:00. What time is he finished? If you said 5:00, you're right.

Speed is often measured in how many miles (kilometers) something can travel in one hour. A kid on a bike usually travels about 5 miles (8 km) per hour.

By the end of first grade, many students can read about 60 words in one minute.

Kate reads a book for half an hour. Half an hour is 30 minutes. Kate reads from 6:00 to 6:30. At 6:30, the long hand points to the 6.

The big hand moves 30 minutes when it moves from 12 to 6.

Juan's cookies need to bake for ten minutes. It takes five minutes for the minute hand to move from one number to the next.

The minute hand is on the 12. Juan puts the cookies in the oven. He counts the minutes: 1, 2, 3, 4, 5. The minute hand is on the 1 after five minutes. He counts 6, 7, 8, 9, 10. After ten minutes, the minute hand is on the 2. The cookies are done. Yum!

Most cookies take 8 to 10 minutes to bake.

Activity

Measuring Time by Fives

There are five minutes between numbers on the clock. Practice measuring time by five minutes. Use your practice clock from the first activity.

1. Think of things that take you 5, 10, 15, 20, or 30 minutes to do.
2. Write them on index cards.
3. Shuffle the cards. Put them face down in a pile.
4. Choose a card. Move your clock hands that many minutes.
5. Keep practicing until all the cards are done.

A Time for Every Activity

School children in the United States finish eating their lunch in about 7 to 10 minutes.

There are 24 hours in one day. This means the little hand points to each number on the clock twice a day. There is nine o'clock each morning and again each evening. We use **a.m.** and **p.m.** to tell them apart. We use a.m. when a time is between **midnight** and **noon**.

It's important for kids to get between 9 and 11 hours of sleep every night.

We use p.m. for times between noon and midnight. At twelve o'clock noon, it is lunchtime! At twelve o'clock midnight, it is dark. You're asleep at midnight.

Until the 1970s, people in Great Britain could hire someone to come and **knock** on their door to **wake them**.

The American alarm clock was **invented** in **1787** by Levi Hutchins.

Today, **70 percent** of people in the United States use an alarm clock.

Kids should get at least 60 minutes of exercise each day.

Kate has softball practice on Saturday at 2:00. Today, practice ended at 3:07. How long did Kate play ball? She uses the clock hands to figure it out.

It takes 12 minutes to walk home from the ball field. If Kate leaves the ball field at 3:15, what time will she get home? If you said 3:27, you're right!

Activity

Match That Time!

Juan and Kate made a matching game. You can make your own game, too. Grab a friend and play together. Match the activities to the correct time.

1. Write activities on index cards.
2. Write the time when you do each activity on different cards.
3. Shuffle the activity cards. Put them facedown in one pile.
4. Lay out the time cards faceup.
5. To play, take turns pulling out an activity card. Find the time card that matches that activity.
6. You can use these activities and times or make up your own. Have fun!

Record-Setting Clocks

There are many record-setting clocks in the United States. Some of these are the largest or most accurate in the nation, or even in the world.

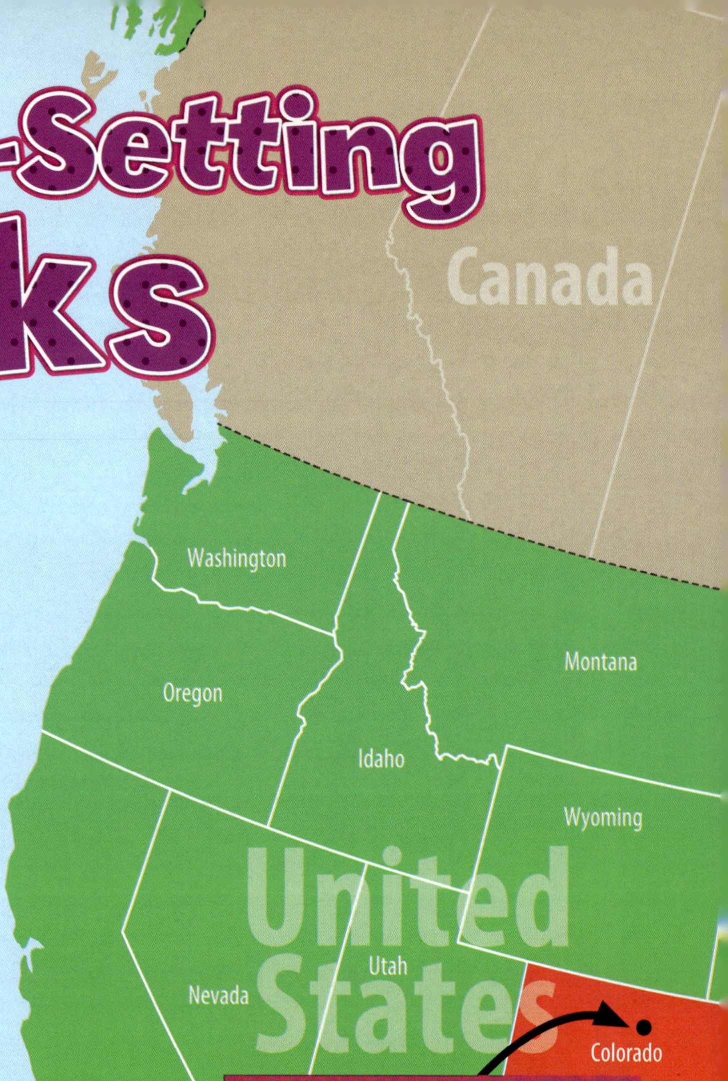

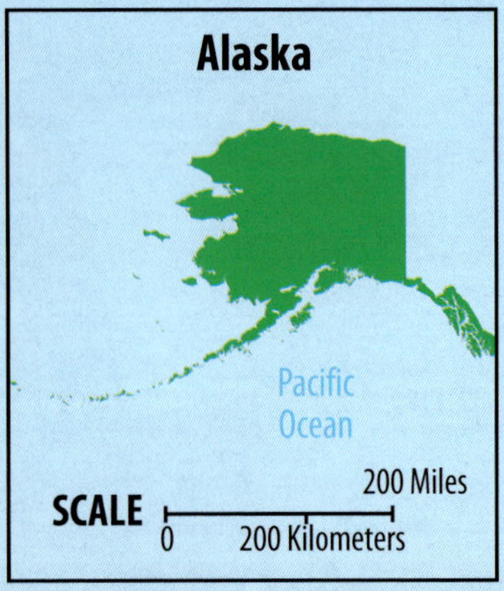

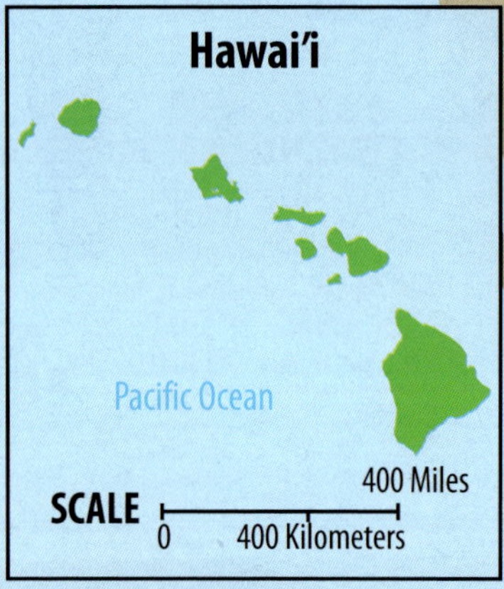

National Institute of Standards and Technology
Boulder, Colorado

Scientists in Colorado made the most accurate clock in the United States, called the **atomic clock**. It will stay on time for about 15 billion years. Official U.S. time is based off the atomic clock.

Grand Central Terminal Clock

New York City, New York

One of the best-known clocks in the world sits inside the Grand Central train station. It is worth between $10 and $20 million. More than 750,000 people pass by it every day.

Timex Group USA

Middlebury, Connecticut

Timex is one of the country's biggest watchmakers. It was founded in 1854. The company now sells more than 300 different styles of watches.

Philadelphia City Hall Clock

Philadelphia, Pennsylvania

Philadelphia City Hall was once one of the tallest buildings in the world. Its clock tower has four of the largest clock faces in the United States. Each is 26 feet (8 m) across.

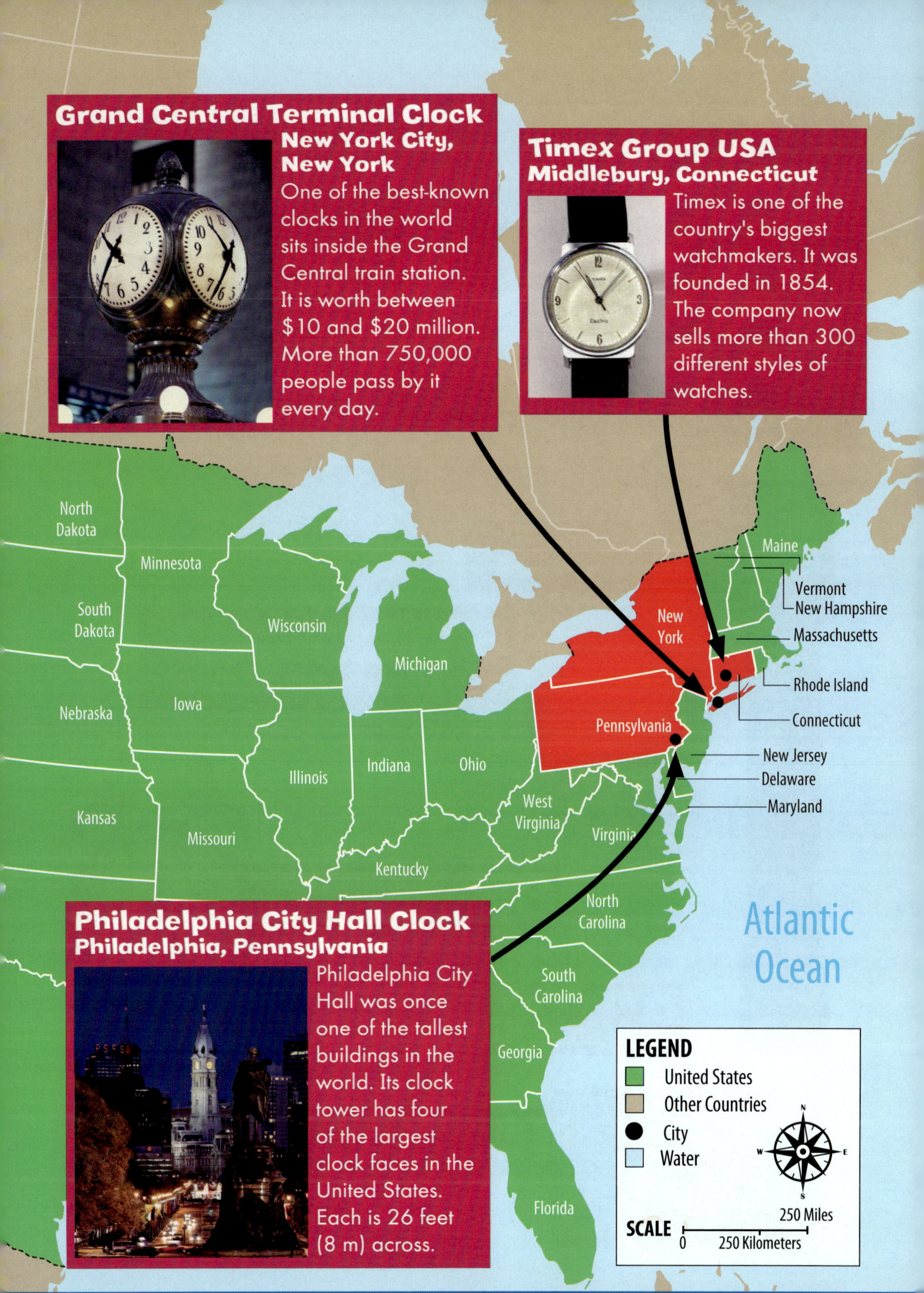

Quiz

1 What are clocks with faces and hands called?

2 What are clocks with only numbers called?

3 Where was the first mechanical watch made?

4 On an analog clock, which hand points to the hour?

5 How many minutes are in one hour?

6 On an analog clock, how many minutes does the big hand move when it moves from 12 to 6?

7 How many hours are there in a day?

8 When did Levi Hutchins invent the alarm clock?

9 What percent of people use an alarm clock?

10 For how long will the atomic clock in Colorado stay on time?

Answers: 1. Analog clocks **2.** Digital clocks **3.** Germany
4. 4. The short hand **5.** 60 **6.** 30 minutes
7. 24 **8.** 1787 **9.** 70 **10.** 15 billion years

Key Words

a.m.: before noon; between midnight and noon

analog: a type of clock with a face and hands

atomic clock: a clock that measures the movement of very small particles called atoms

digital: a type of clock with numbers separated by a colon

hourglasses: devices for measuring time made of clear containers that have thick parts at both ends and narrow spaces in between through which sand pours

midnight: twelve o'clock at nighttime

noon: twelve o'clock in the daytime

p.m.: after noon; between noon and midnight

sundial: a tool for telling time that has a plate with markings like a clock and an arm that casts a shadow onto the plate

units: standard amounts that are used to measure things

Index

LIGHTBOX

SUPPLEMENTARY RESOURCES

Click on the plus icon found in the bottom left corner of each spread to open additional teacher resources.

- Download and print the book's quizzes and activities
- Access curriculum correlations
- Explore additional web applications that enhance the Lightbox experience

LIGHTBOX DIGITAL TITLES
Packed full of integrated media

VIDEOS

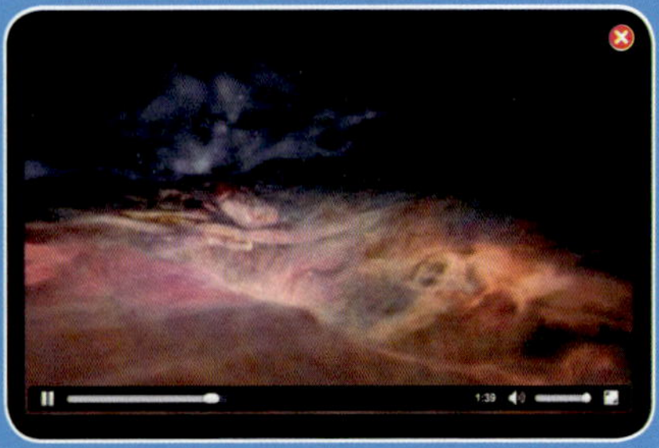

INTERACTIVE MAPS

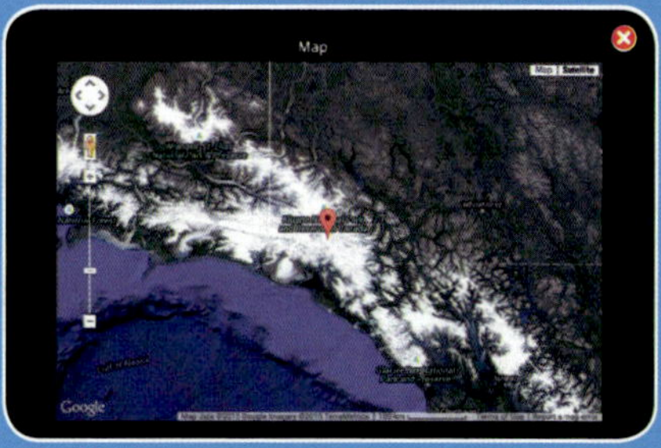

WEBLINKS

SLIDESHOWS

QUIZZES

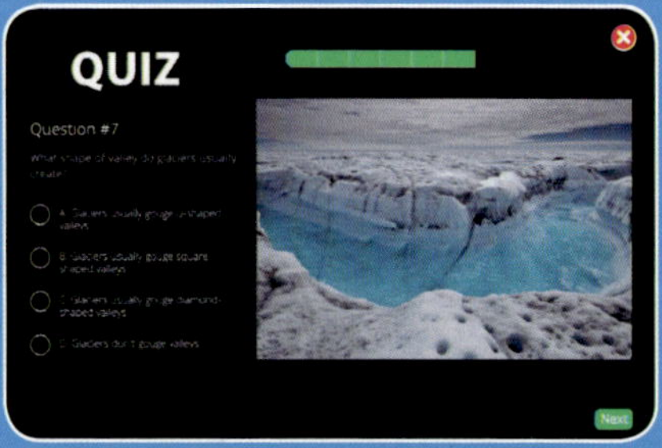

OPTIMIZED FOR

- ✔ TABLETS
- ✔ WHITEBOARDS
- ✔ COMPUTERS
- ✔ AND MUCH MORE!

Published by Smartbook Media Inc. 350 5th Avenue, 59th Floor New York, NY 10118
Website: www.openlightbox.com

012018
120517

Library of Congress Control Number: 2017960152

ISBN 978-1-5105-3634-0 (hardcover)
ISBN 978-1-5105-3635-7 (multi-user eBook)

Printed in the Brainerd, Minnesota, United States
1 2 3 4 5 6 7 8 9 0 22 21 20 19 18

First published by Cherry Lake in 2014.

Project Coordinator: John Willis
Designer: Ana María Vidal

Every reasonable effort has been made to trace ownership and to obtain permission to reprint copyright material. The publisher would be pleased to have any errors or omissions brought to its attention so that they may be corrected in subsequent printings.

The publisher acknowledges Alamy, Getty Images, and iStock as the primary image suppliers for this title.